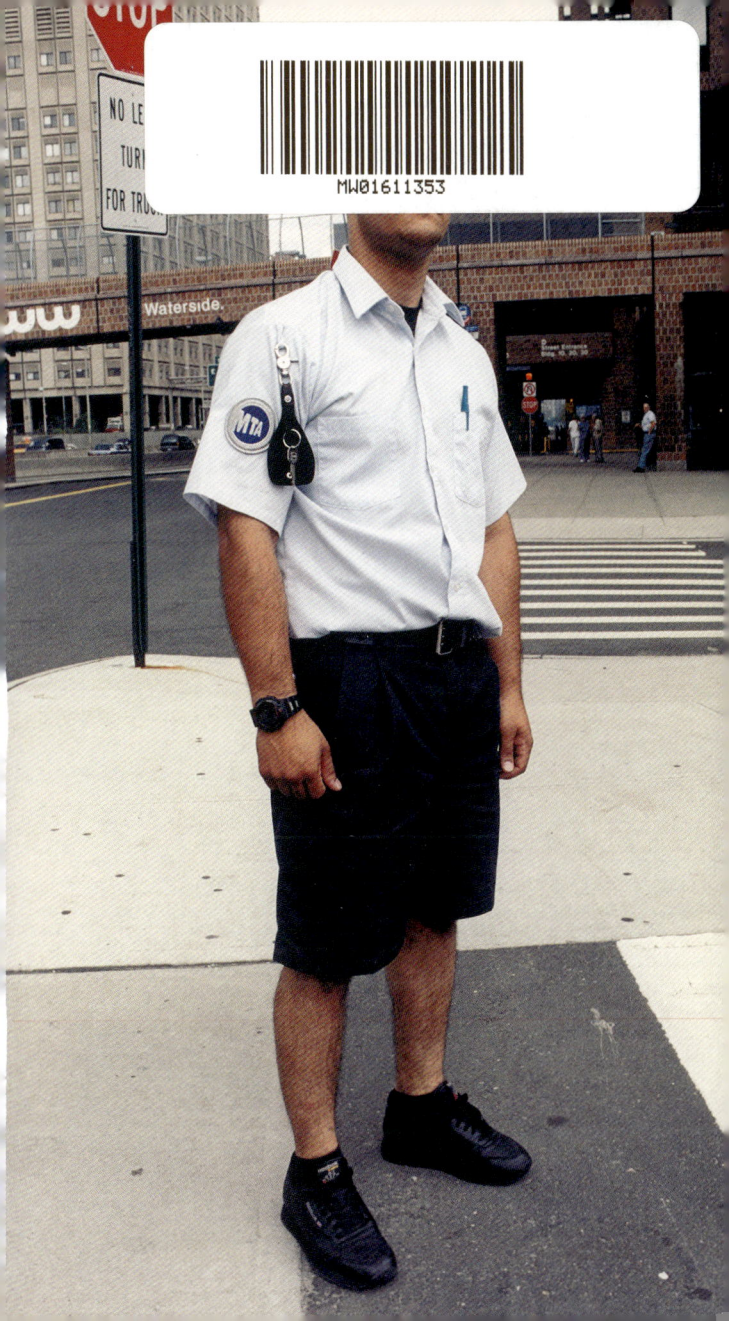

#1514

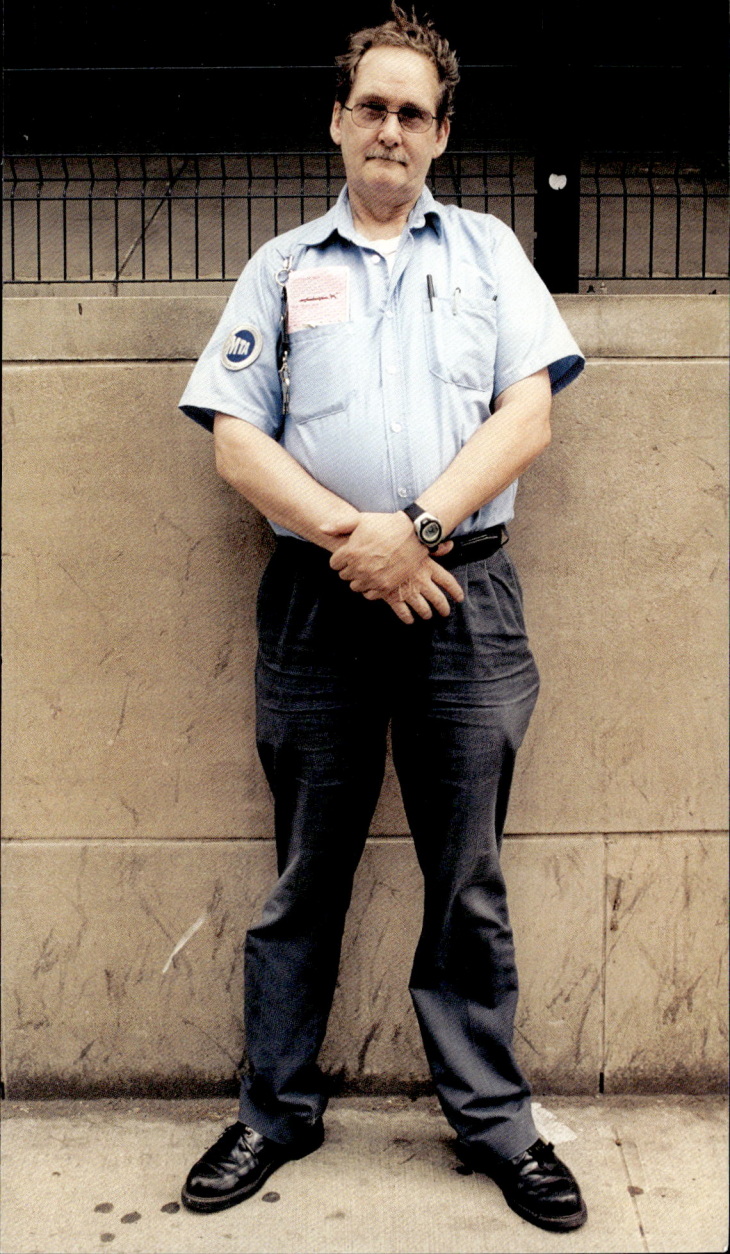

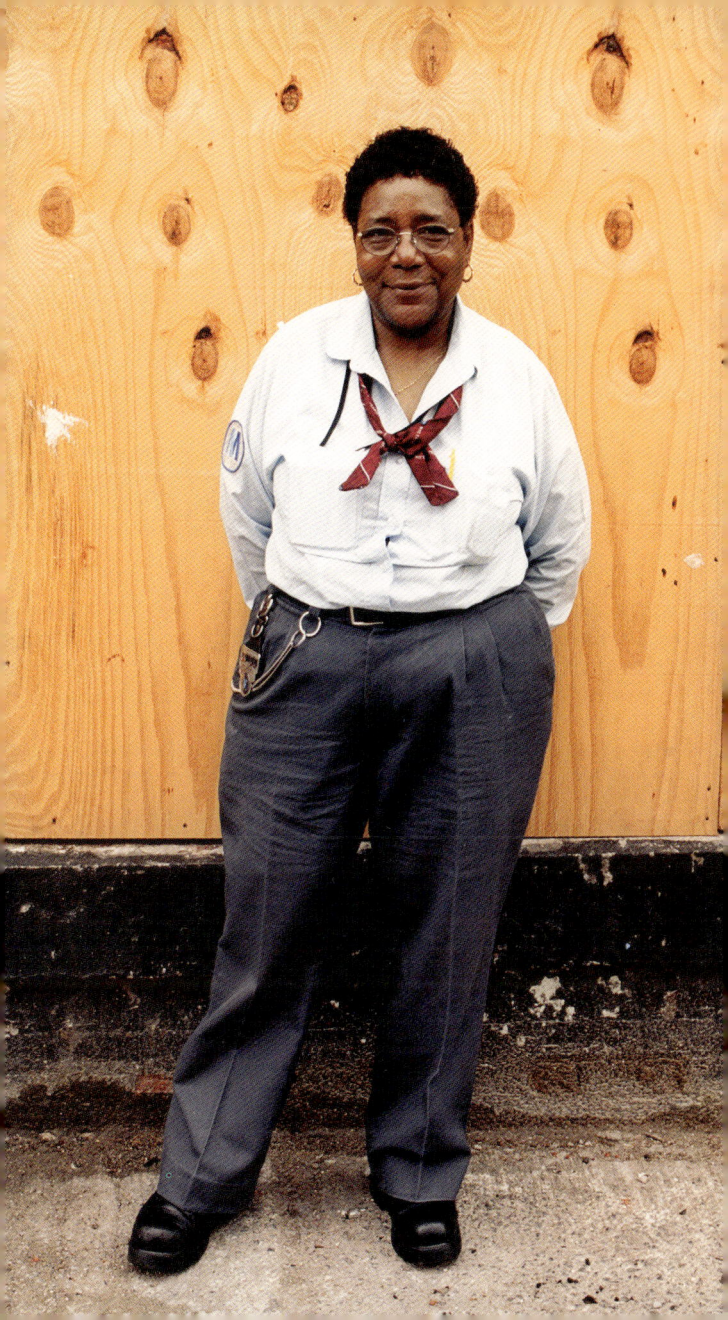

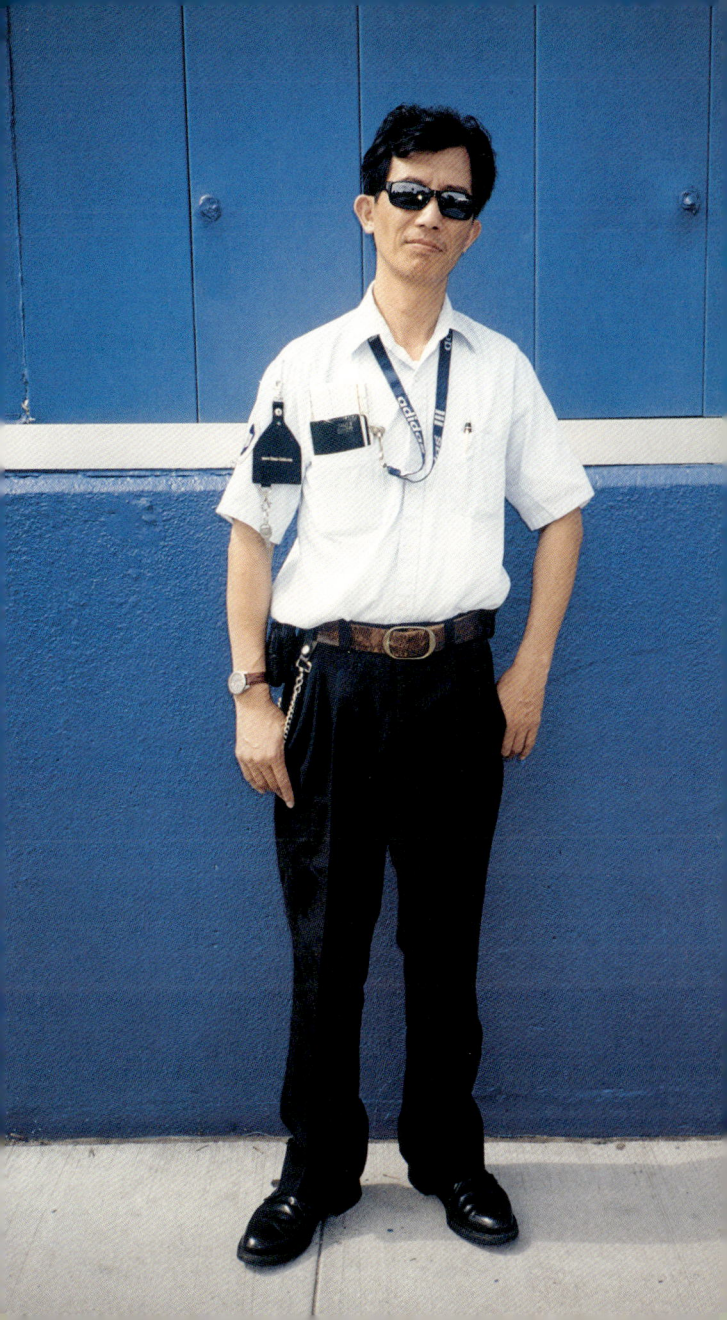

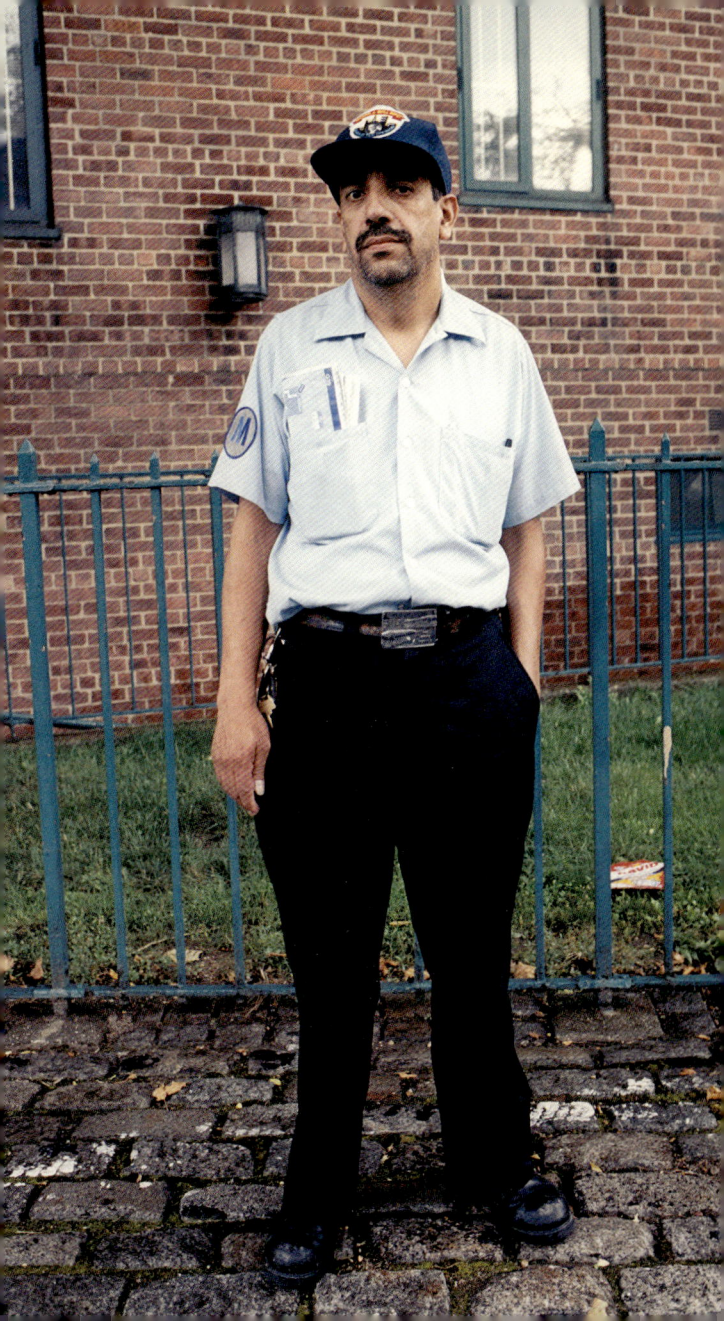

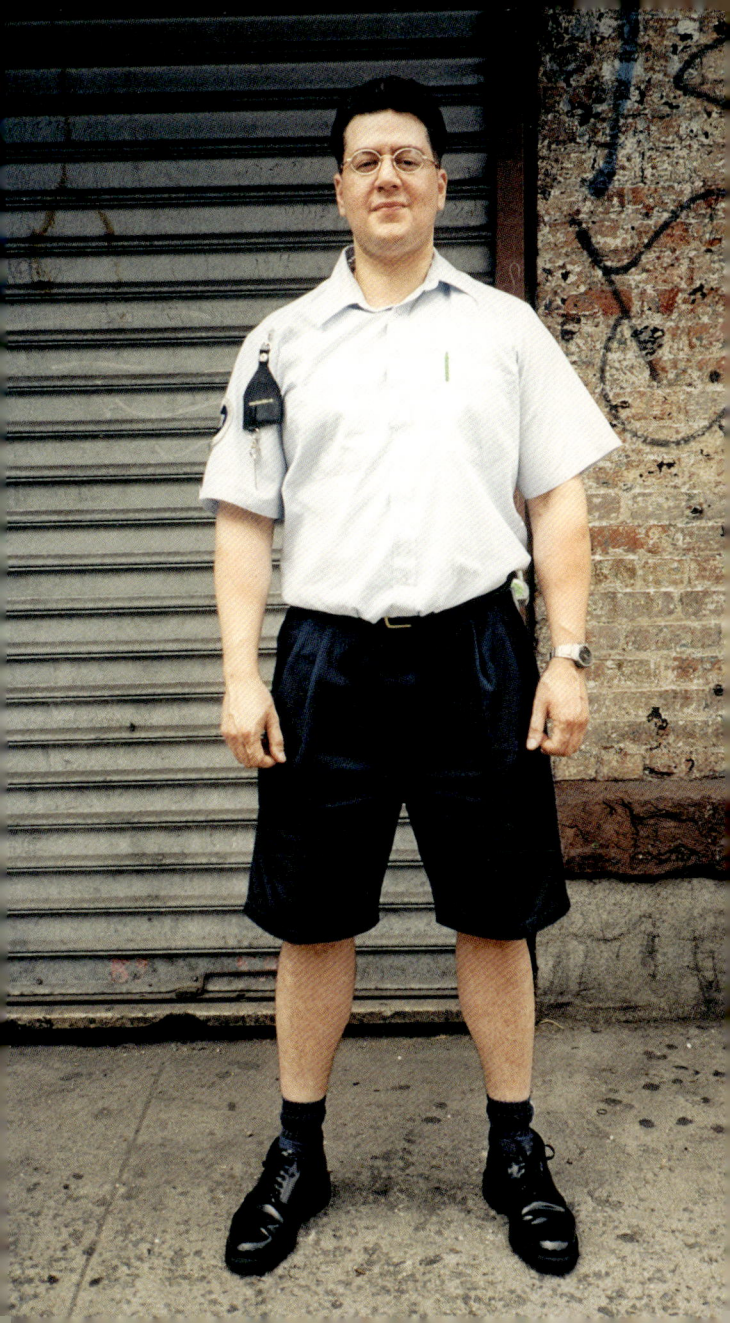

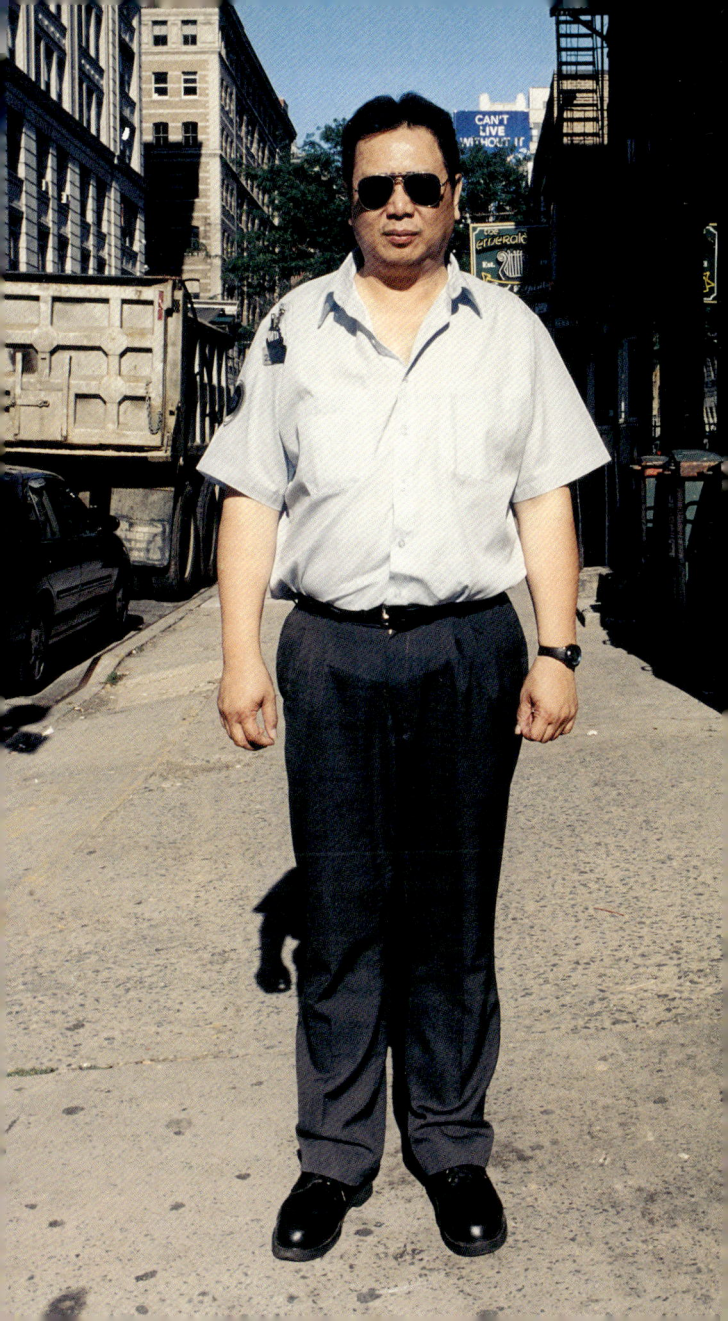

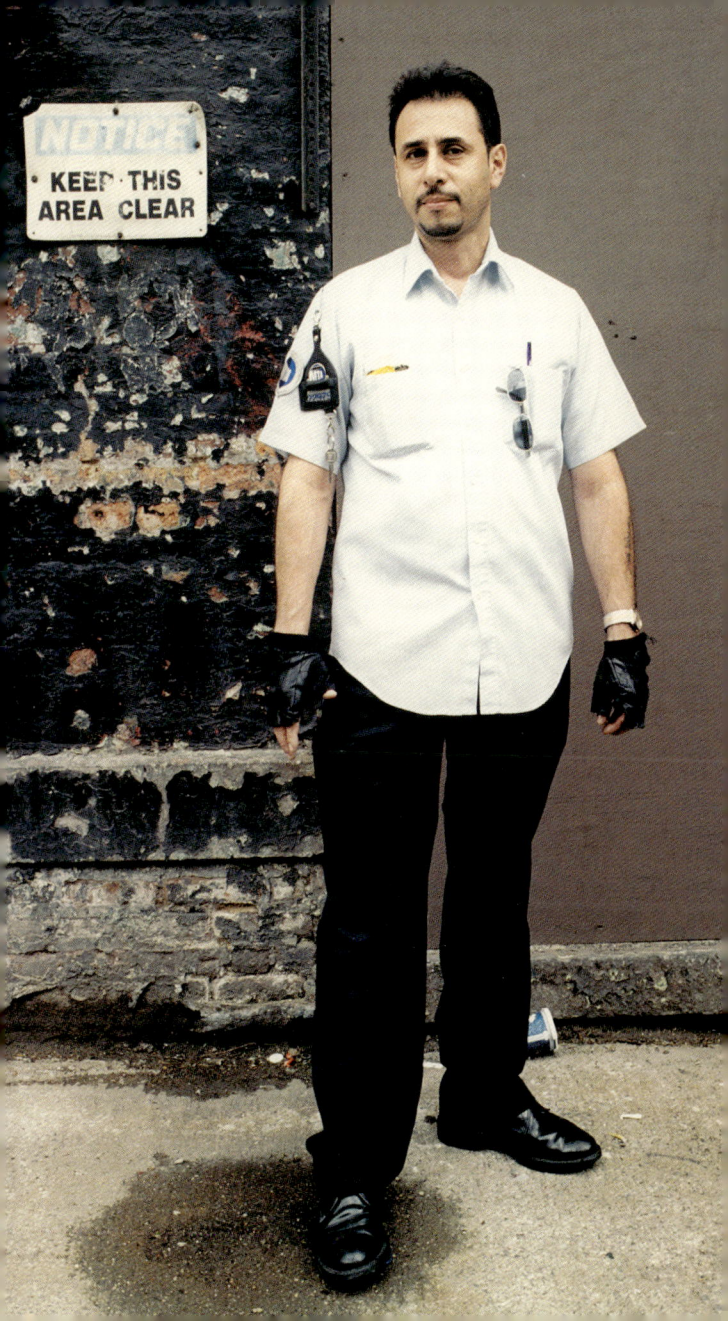

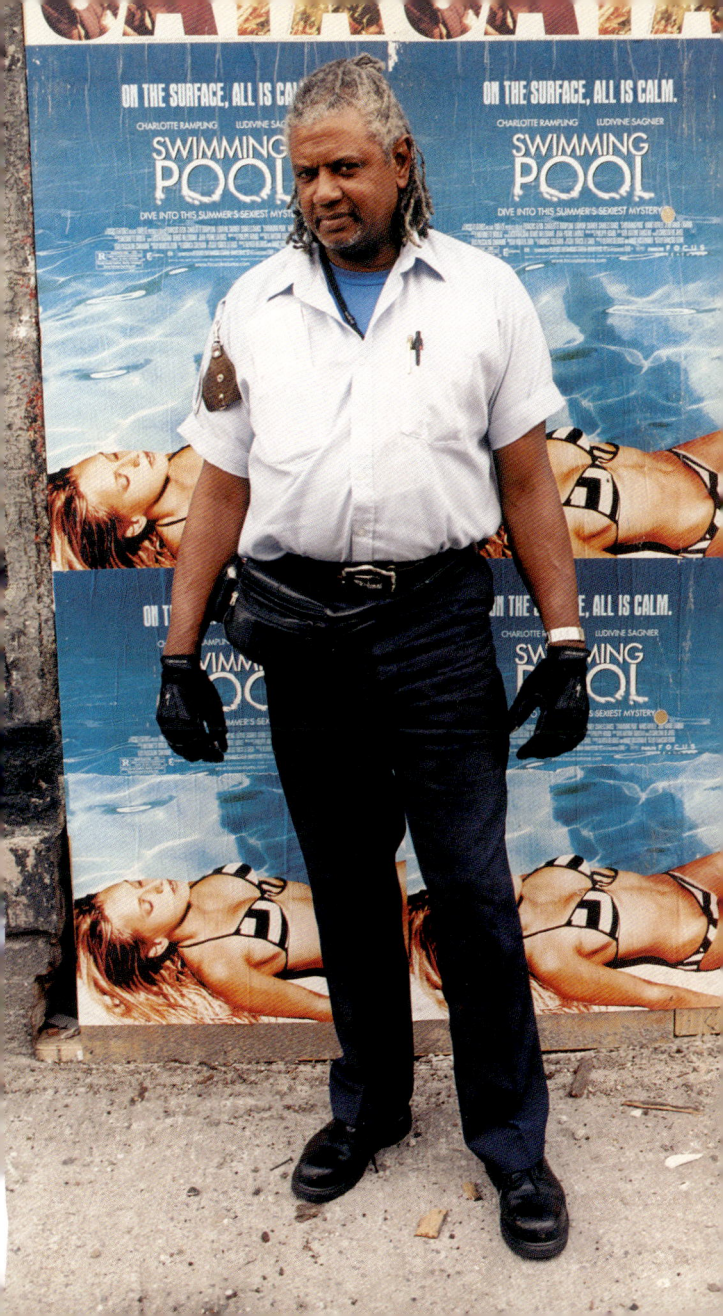

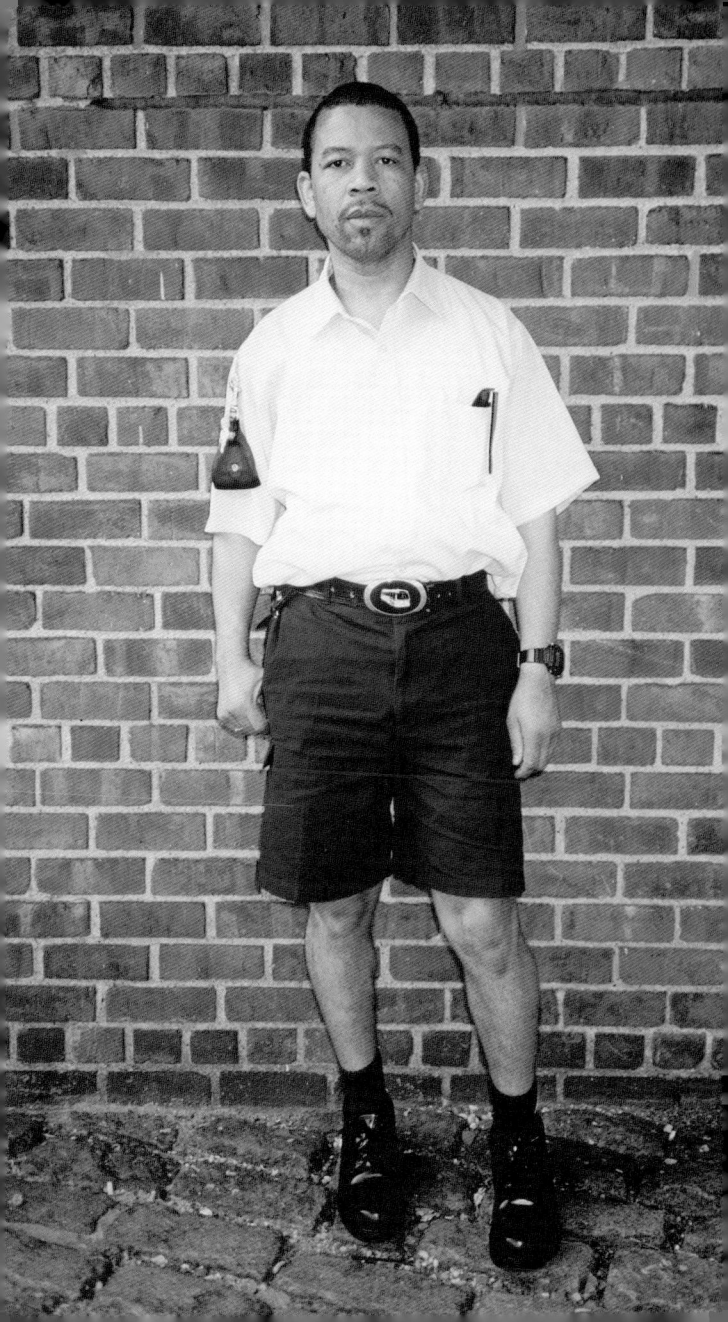

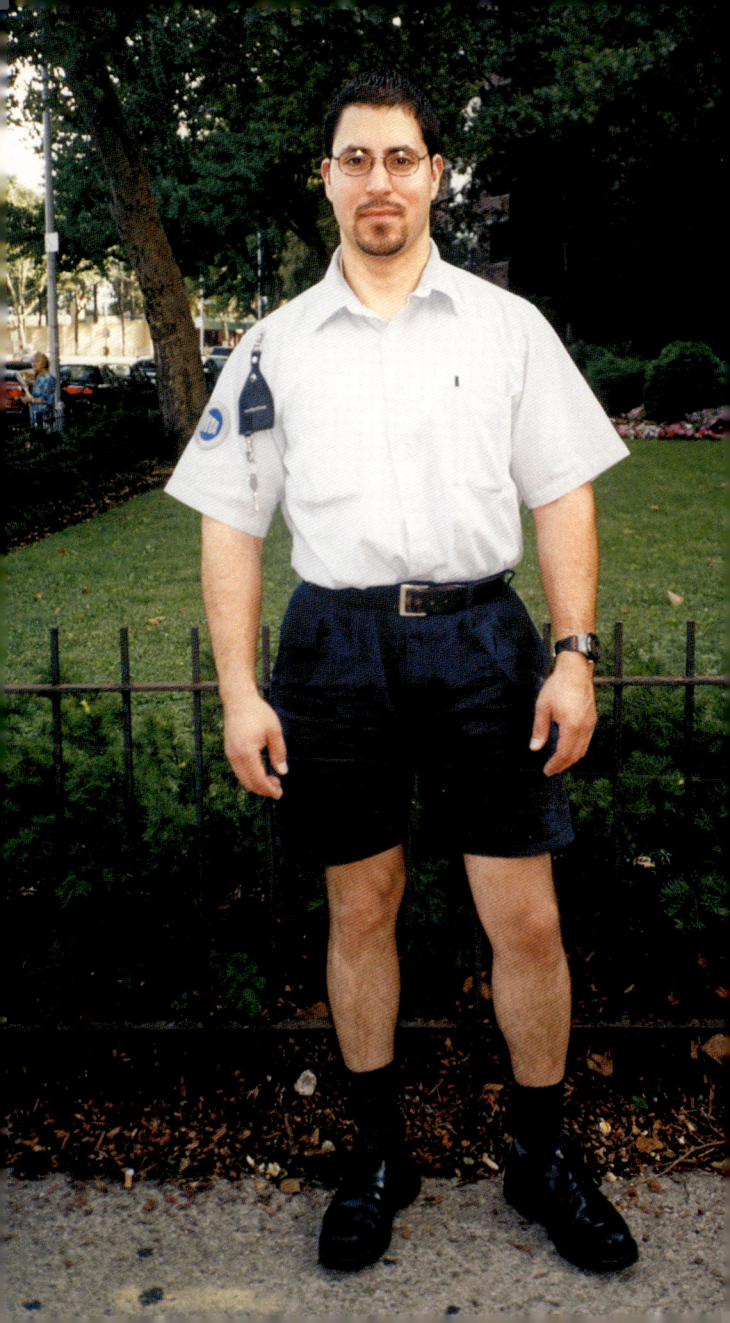

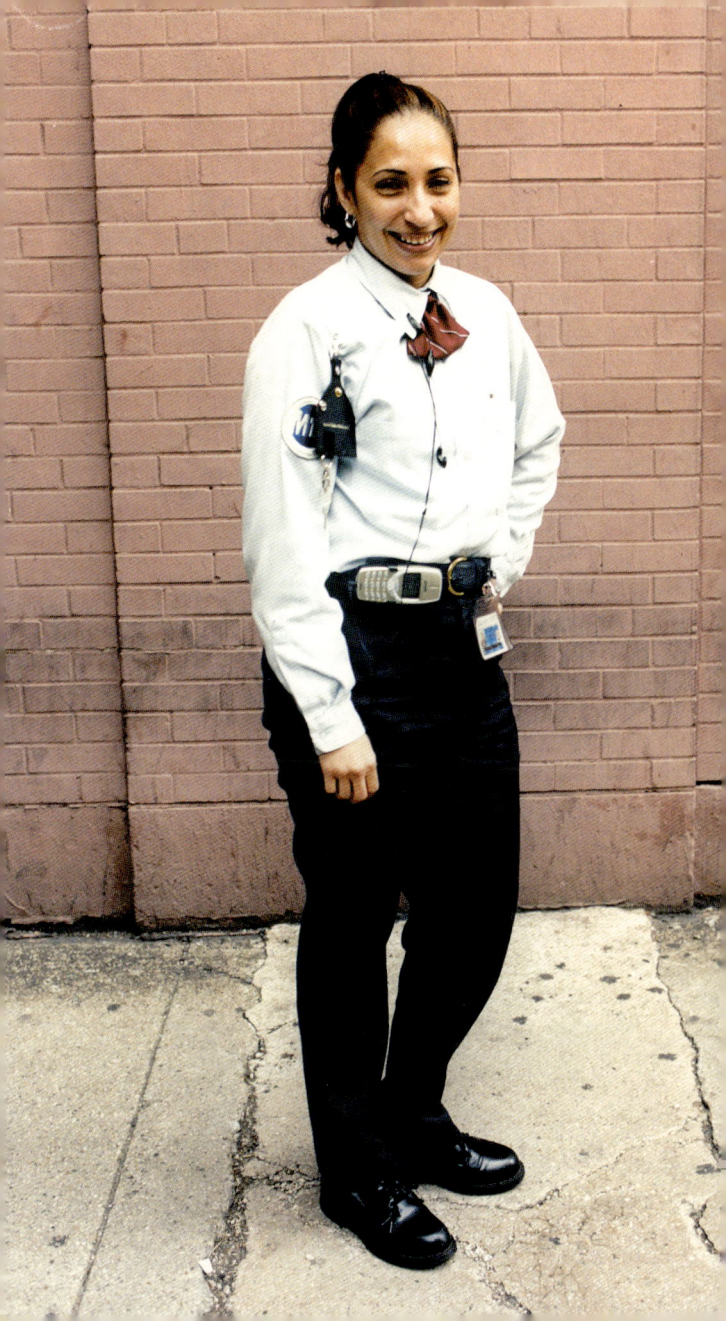

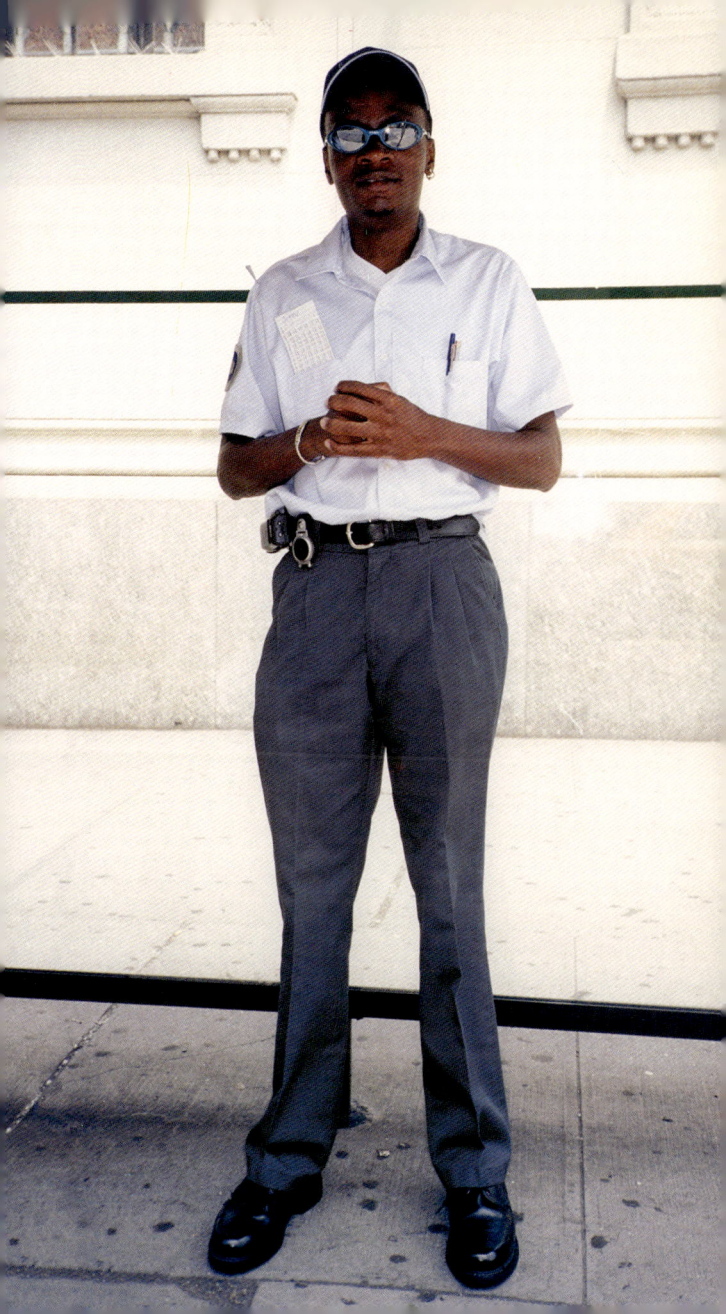

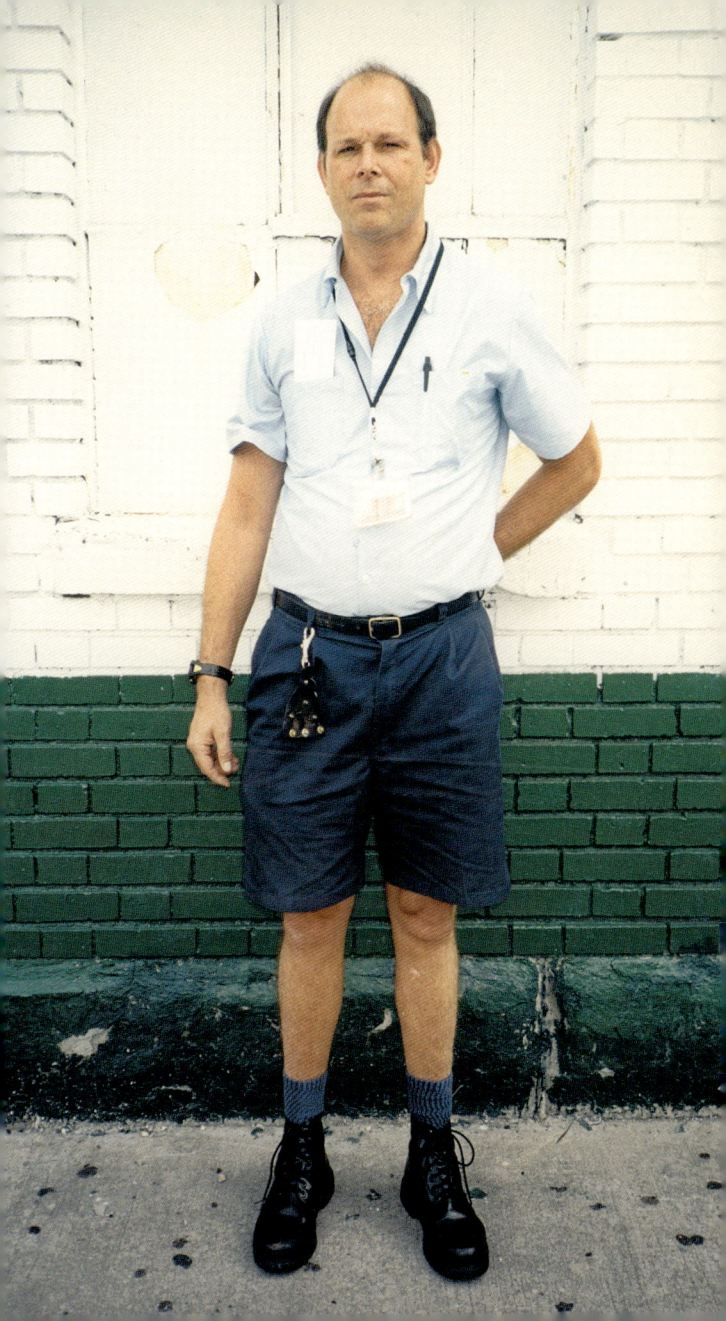

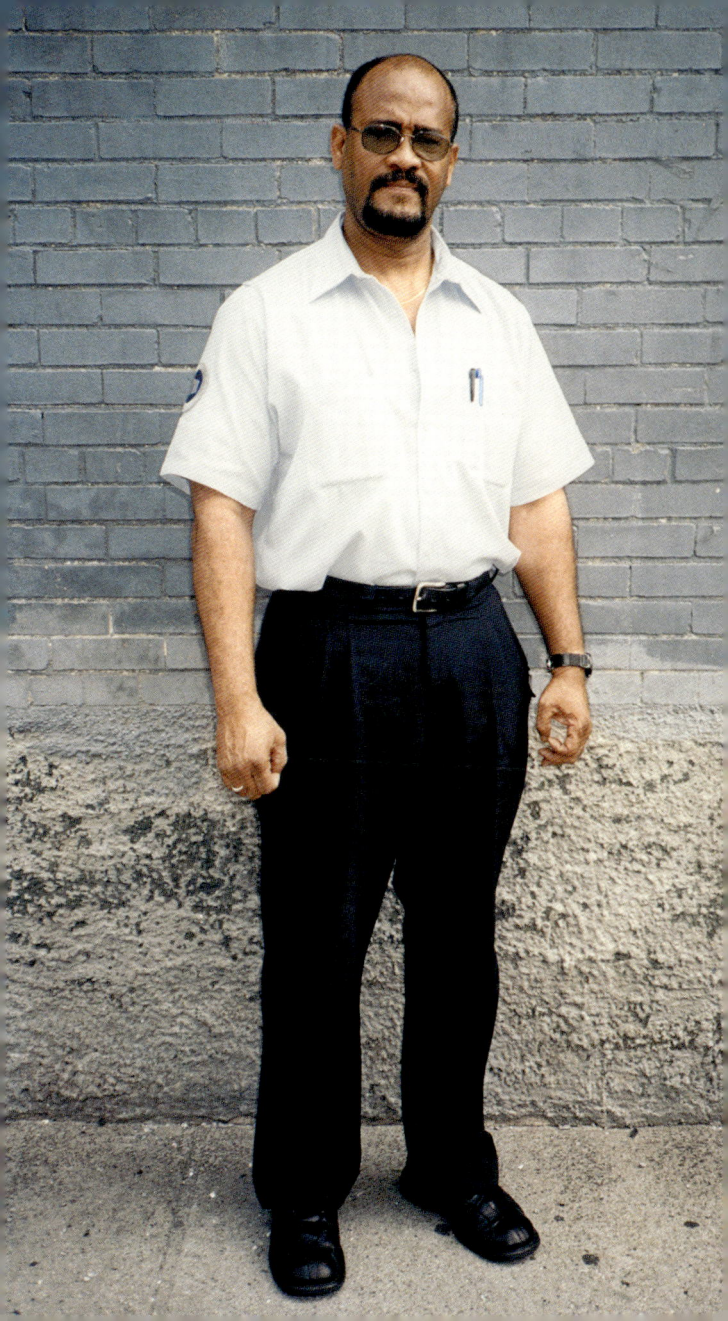

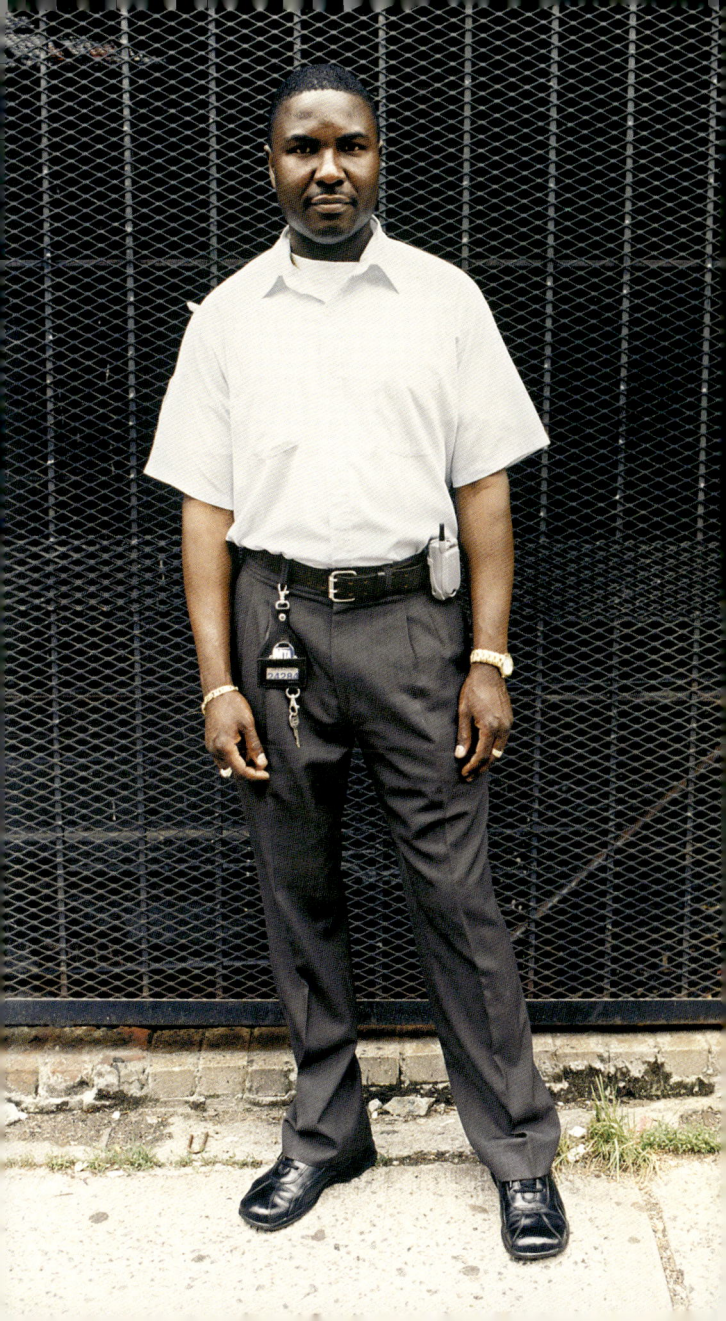

**Jennifer Bornstein
How to Ride the Bus**

Four Corners Books

IN CASE YOU DON'T USUALLY take the bus around New York City, I highly recommend it—it's cheap and air-conditioned and you get to sit next to, and sometimes touch, people you don't know. There's plenty to see, inside and out: street action, fashion statements, and most of all, people. Not that people are more interesting on the bus than off. But on the bus there's extra time to meet them, because the bus inevitably takes forever. There's always an enormous traffic jam, or a passenger with elaborate demands. It's faster to get off and walk. Which is what I usually end up doing.

I know about the bus because for two years I had a job that required me to travel around New York City, and the bus was my preferred means of transportation. I took at least two and sometimes as many as twenty buses a day. Once in a while I took a cab. My boss paid all transportation expenses, so there was no reason not to. But I wasn't in a hurry. I didn't really care when I got to where I was supposed to be going. So usually the bus worked fine.

There's pleasure in having too much time, especially when everyone around seems to have none.

There's also pleasure in not working, but it's nothing compared to the pleasure of *not being on the job* when actually *on the job*. All that time saved by not working when you're supposed to be working leaves an enormous amount of time to spend on other things, such as trips to the library, or simply the quiet action of bus-riding around Manhattan, documenting bus routes while busy doing something that, by definition, requires *no documentation*.

Say you're on the corner of 53rd and 3rd. If you're thinking of going uptown, the M103 bus will take you up 3rd all the way to 125th. Stay on the bus and it'll turn around and go back down Lexington, past Payard Patisserie at East 73rd, past the Gramercy Hotel, past St Mark's Bookshop at East 9th, until 3rd Avenue turns into the Bowery and crosses Bleecker. This trip certainly uses up a lot of time. You can break it up with a stop at the New York Public Library at 42nd Street, or look out the window, or look at the objects that the people sitting around you are carrying. Or, to go deeper into the east side, take the M15. It starts at the tip of Battery Park City, which is impossible to access by subway, and runs up 1st Avenue to 125th Street near the Triborough Bridge. Then it turns west for a block and heads back down 2nd Avenue to 1st Street, turns south onto Allen, and goes back down to Battery Park City. The M42 and M23 go all the way to 12th Avenue, which is rare. The M23 also intersects the M5, which runs down 5th Avenue towards Washington Square Park (which was used as a hanging ground during the American Revolution), past the NYU dorm where "Felicity" lived, turns east on Houston and then loops up Broadway, crossing 3rd Street where the Broadway Central Hotel used to be, which used to house the Mercer Arts Center, where punk bands used to play before the building collapsed in 1973, killing four people. Some buses go deep east *and* west. The M5 starts on the east side but runs across Houston to 6th Avenue, turns up 6th and runs north to Central Park West, past the West 11th Street block between 5th and 6th Avenues where the Weathermen blew themselves up at #18. The M16 turns south on 2nd Avenue from 34th Street and loops down to 23rd, goes all the way to the East River on 23rd (past the Asser Levy Pool, which is free during the summer), and then turns north and runs along the FDR, making a stop at Waterside Plaza before heading back up to 34th Street.

If you're on the west side near 14th Street and want to go to the Lower East Side, take the M14D (not to be confused with the M14A, which runs down Avenue A to the East River near Grand Street—also good, but not the M14D). The M14D starts at the Chelsea Piers at 18th and West Street and runs across West 14th Street, past Duchamp's studio at #210 (upstairs), past the Strand Bookstore, to Avenue D, the FDR, and the Williamsburg Bridge. When you get to the end of the line at Delancey and Columbia, walk two blocks south to Madison, turn right on Madison and walk seven blocks south to East Broadway. Cross the street and transfer to the B51, which takes you across the Manhattan

Bridge all the way to Brooklyn. Or, cross back and catch the northbound M15, which takes you back up Allen Street and back up 1st Avenue. Get off on West 72nd and catch the westbound M72, going through the Upper East Side, past the cafe that used to serve lime-blossom tea, then turning south on 5th Avenue and running along Central Park before entering the park near the zoo, emerging on the other side near West 66th Street. The bus turns north on Central Park West, makes a left on West 72nd, passes the Dakota (where Mia Farrow and John Cassavetes lived in *Rosemary's Baby*), and crosses the corner of West End Avenue and West 70th, which is near Ungano's, the basement night club at 210 West 70th where Iggy Pop once took out his penis during a show and put it on top of a speaker and let it vibrate around.

This is a long trip, which leaves more time to meet bus drivers. Strategically, the best way to meet drivers is to travel to the end of the route, when people disappear and drivers grow talkative. Or you can hang out at the turn-arounds, where drivers take breaks between shifts.

If you have an entire day to kill, take the M4 to the Cloisters on West 200th Street. Or, take the M1, M2, or M3 up Park Avenue South through the junction at Madison Avenue to the Upper East Side. Get off on East 84th and visit the 18th century French period rooms on the first floor of the Metropolitan Museum. From there, visit the jewels and the Louis Comfort Tiffany room. Wander outside and through the park before catching the bus going south on 5th

Avenue, which if you've timed it right won't be during rush hour and will be running empty. Sit on the west side of the bus as it travels south along Central Park for a close-up look at the leaves on trees from 84th to 59th Streets. Or, get off and walk through the park to the Endicott building on the corner of West 81st & Columbus Avenue, which used to be the homeless shelter where the New York Dolls played their first show, on Christmas Eve 1971. From there, catch the M7 down Columbus Avenue, past the turret where Margaret Mead had her office on West 77th Street. Or, walk east to Lexington Avenue and get on a downtown M101, M102, or M103, which will take you to the M23, which will take you to the M6, which will take you to the stop on Canal & 6th Avenue that used to be the place to get off to go to American Fine Arts.

The M42 is swift on 42nd Street, but by the time it gets to 2nd Avenue it slows to a crawl because of traffic near the entrance to the Queens-Midtown Tunnel. That last block alone can take thirty minutes or more. The M20 runs well from the tip of South End Avenue all the way up to Central Park South, but there are three or four blocks on 6th Avenue near the entrance to the Holland Tunnel when it can be motionless. To negotiate this, get off before the traffic areas begin and walk through on foot to catch a bus emerging on the other side. If you're not in a hurry, however, stay on the bus to observe the people sitting around you. If they're annoying, you know for a fact they'll vanish in a few minutes. If they're interesting you can talk to them. If talking gets boring you can get off.

GOOD BUSES:

M11 (Travels up the west side relatively quickly.)

M23 (Slow, but accesses neighborhoods the subway
doesn't, like the far eastern sections of Kips Bay
or the far western sections of Chelsea.)

M15 (Comes every five minutes.)

BAD BUSES:

M14 (Takes forever–try the L train instead. Exception:
the C and D lines run through the East Village and
into the Lower East Side, which is convenient.)

M21 (Houston Street bus–slow schedule and stops
running at midnight. Drivers tend to be angry.)

For Giovanni Intra, bus rider

Thanks to Tim Blum, Gavin Brown, Corinna Durland, Richard Embray, Cornelia Grassi, Francesca Grassi, Elinor Jansz, John Kelsey, Martin Lee, Tony Manzella, Jeff Poe, Willem de Rooij, Ali Subotnick, Silke Taprogge, Kelly Taylor, Lincoln Tobier, and Christopher Williams.

Published by Four Corners Books, London
www.fourcornersbooks.co.uk

Copyright © Four Corners Books and Jennifer Bornstein, 2007
All photographs and text copyright © Jennifer Bornstein, 2003

Design: Lincoln Tobier
Printing: Balding + Mansell
Color separations: Echelon
Printing production: Martin Lee

Distributed in the UK by Art Data www.artdata.co.uk
ISBN 978-0-9545025-3-9